Terrible Things

EVE BUNTING

Terrible Things

An Allegory of the Holocaust

ILLUSTRATED BY
Stephen Gammell

The Jewish Publication Society

Philadelphia

The first JPS printing of this book was an Edward E. Elson Edition
and was made possible by a gift in memory of Louis Elson.

Library of Congress Cataloging in Publication Data

Bunting, Eve, 1928-
    Terrible Things: an allegory of the Holocaust / Eve Bunting :
illustrated by Stephen Gammell.
            p. cm.
    "This book was originally published in 1980 by Harper & Row."
    Summary: In this allegory, the author's reaction to the Holocaust, the animals of the forest
are carried away, one type after another, by the Terrible Things, not realizing that if perhaps
they would all stick together and not look the other way, such terrible things might not happen.

Cloth, ISBN 0-8276-0325-8
Paperback, ISBN 0-8276-0507-2

[1. Animals-Fiction.   2. Allegories.]   I. Gammell, Stephen,

ill.   II. Title.
PZ7.B91527Ts 1989
[E]–dc19   89-2163
                                                                        CIP
                                                                        AC

            09 10 11 12 13 14   20 21 22 23 24 25 26 27 28

To My Dear Friend
Mary Sullivan

In Europe, during World War II, many people looked
the other way while terrible things happened. They
pretended not to know that their neighbors were
being taken away and locked in concentration camps.
They pretended not to hear their cries for help. The Nazis
killed millions of Jews and others in the Holocaust.
If everyone had stood together at the first sign of evil
would this have happened?

Standing up for what you know is right is not always
easy. Especially if the one you face is bigger and
stronger than you. It is easier to look the other way.
But if you do, terrible things can happen.

—E.B.

The clearing in the woods was home to the small forest creatures. The birds and squirrels shared the trees. The rabbits and porcupines shared the shade beneath the trees and the frogs and fish shared the cool brown waters of the forest pond. They were content.

Until the day the Terrible Things came.

Little Rabbit saw their terrible shadows before he saw them. They stopped at the edge of the clearing and their shadows blotted out the sun.

"We have come for every creature with feathers on its back," the Terrible Things thundered.

"We don't have feathers," the frogs said.

"Nor we," said the squirrels.

"Nor we," said the porcupines.

"Nor we," said the rabbits.

The little fish leaped from the water to show the shine of their scales, but the birds twittered nervously in the tops of the trees. Feathers! They rose in the air, then screamed away into the blue of the sky.

But the Terrible Things had brought their
terrible nets and they flung them high and
caught the birds and carried them away.

The other forest creatures talked nervously among themselves.

"Those birds were always too noisy," Old Porcupine said. "Good riddance, I say."

"There's more room in the trees now," the squirrels said.

"Why did the Terrible Things want the birds?" Little Rabbit asked. "What's wrong with feathers?"

"We mustn't ask," Big Rabbit said. "The Terrible Things don't need a reason. Just be glad it wasn't us they wanted."

Now there were no birds to sing in the
clearing. But life went on almost as before.
Until the day the Terrible Things came back.

Little Rabbit heard the thump of their terrible feet before they came into sight.

"We have come for every bushy-tailed creature who lives in the clearing," the Terrible Things thundered.

"We have no tails," the frogs said.

"Nor do we. Not real tails," the porcupines said.

The little fish leaped from the water to show the smooth shine of their finned tails and the rabbits turned their rumps so the Terrible Things could see for themselves.

"Our tails are round and furry," they said. "By no means are they bushy."

The squirrels chittered their fear and ran high into the treetops. But the Terrible Things swung their terrible nets higher than the squirrels could run and wider than the squirrels could leap and they caught them all and carried them away.

"Those squirrels were greedy," Big Rabbit said. "Always storing away things for themselves. Never sharing."

"But why did the Terrible Things take them away?" Little Rabbit asked. "Do the Terrible Things want the clearing for themselves?"

"No. They have their own place," Big Rabbit said. "But the Terrible Things don't need a reason. Just mind your own business, Little Rabbit. We don't want them to get mad at us."

Now there were no birds to sing or squirrels to chitter in the trees. But life in the clearing went on almost as before. Until the day the Terrible Things came again.

Little Rabbit heard the rumble of their terrible voices.

"We have come for every creature that swims," the Terrible Things thundered.

"Oh, we can't swim," the rabbits said quickly.

"And we can't swim," the porcupines said.

The frogs dived deep in the forest pool and ripples spiraled like corkscrews on the dark, brown water. The little fish darted this way and that in streaks of silver. But the Terrible Things threw their terrible nets down into the depths and they dragged up the dripping frogs and the shimmering fish and carried them away.

"Why did the Terrible Things take them?"
Little Rabbit asked. "What did the frogs and the
fish do to them?"

"Probably nothing," Big Rabbit said. "But the
Terrible Things don't need a reason. Many
creatures dislike frogs. Lumpy, slimy things. And
fish are so cold and unfriendly. They never talk
to any of us."

Now there were no birds to sing, no squirrels
to chitter, no frogs to croak, no fish to play in
the forest pool. A nervous silence filled the
clearing. But life went on almost as usual. Until
the day the Terrible Things came back.

Little Rabbit smelled their terrible smell before they came into sight. The rabbits and the porcupines looked everywhere, except at each other.

"We have come for every creature that sprouts quills," the Terrible Things thundered.

The rabbits stopped quivering. "We don't have quills," they said, fluffing their soft, white fur.

The porcupines bristled with all their strength.
But the Terrible Things covered them with the
curl of their terrible nets and the porcupines
hung in them like flies in a spider's web as the
Terrible Things carried them away.

"Those porcupines always were bad tempered," Big Rabbit said shakily. "Prickly, stickly things!"

This time Little Rabbit didn't ask why. By now he knew that the Terrible Things didn't need a reason. The smell still filled the clearing, though the Terrible Things had gone.

"I liked it better when there were all kinds of creatures in our clearing," he said. "And I think we should move. What if the Terrible Things come back?"

"Nonsense," Big Rabbit said. "Why should we move? This has always been our home. And the Terrible Things won't come back. We are the White Rabbits. It couldn't happen to us."

As day followed peaceful day Little Rabbit
thought Big Rabbit must be right. Until the day
the Terrible Things came back.

Little Rabbit saw the terrible gleam of their terrible eyes through the forest darkness. And he smelled again the terrible smell.

"We have come for any creature that is white," the Terrible Things thundered.

"There are no white creatures here but us," Big Rabbit said.

"We have come for you," the Terrible Things said.

The rabbits scampered in every direction. "Help!" they screamed. "Somebody help!" But there was no one left to help. And the big, circling nets dropped over them and the Terrible Things carried them away.

All but Little Rabbit, who was little enough to hide in a pile of rocks by the pond and smart enough to stay so still that the Terrible Things thought he was a rock himself.

When they had all gone Little Rabbit crept
into the middle of the empty clearing. I should
have tried to help the other rabbits, he thought.
If only we creatures had stuck together, it could
have been different.

Sadly, Little Rabbit left the clearing. He'd go tell other forest creatures about the Terrible Things. He hoped someone would listen.